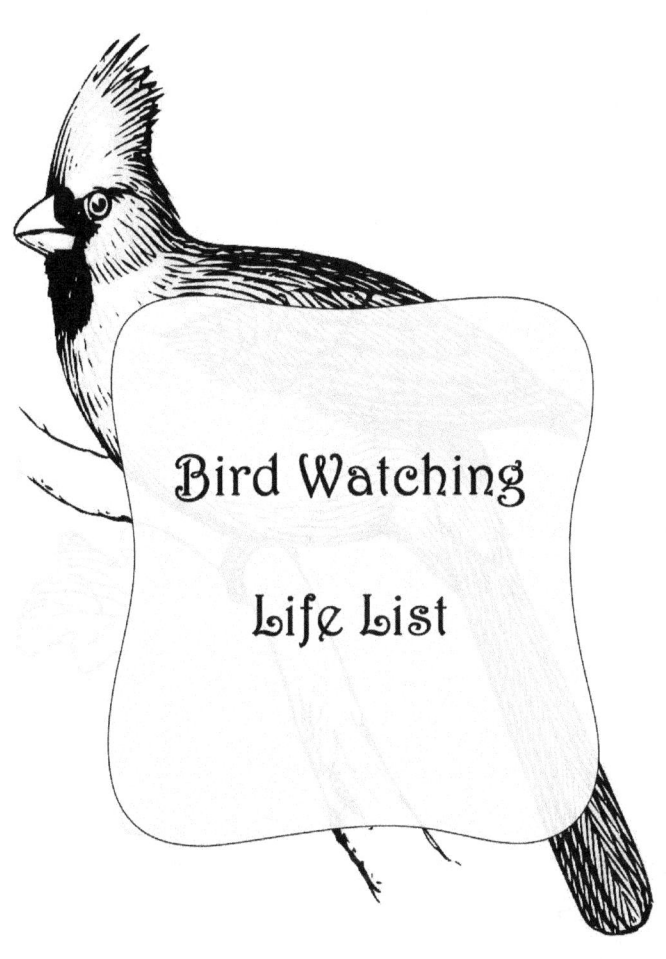

Bird Watching

Life List

Kim Marie Johnson

SOMETHING BEAUTIFUL is about to happen... ©

Bird Watching Life List

Design:
Kim Marie Johnson

Cover Photo:
Designed by Kim Marie Johnson
Bird drawings from www.openclipart.com

For more information contact: Kim Marie Johnson
kmjdesign@elberton.net

ISBN 13: 978-1537068558
ISBN 10: 1537068555

This Life List

Belongs To

Introduction

Bird Watching is one of the most enjoyable, stress-relieving hobbies you will ever find.

The Bird Watching Life List provides a space for an ongoing record of the birds you observe. Transfer notes from your field journal. The Bird Watching Life List also includes space for a Yard List, A Trip List, and a Wish List. The novice and experienced bird watcher will enjoy the book format and convenient size of this Life List. It would make a perfect gift for the bird watcher in your life.

Bird watching is an easy hobby to move into. One may begin by simply observing the birds in their own back yard. Don't just look at the bird. Quiet your mind and really observe.

I hope you will enjoy this Bird Watching Life List.

Kim Marie Johnson

Bird Watching Field Journal

Write your notes in your field journal as soon as possible, while they are fresh in your memory. As you become more experienced, referring back to your observation notes will help you to understand what you missed and want to look for in the future.

It is important to record dates, location, and the weather. Record the bird's habitat, behavior, and appearance. Draw or sketch the bird, even if you do not consider yourself an artist, you can capture small details.

If you were on a trip, make note of this and add details. Don't forget to note people who shared this observation with you. If you just met these bird watcher enthusiasts, you will want their contact information.

Your Bird Watching Life List will become a favorite record that you will refer to often as you engage in this life-long pursuit.

Tools of the Bird Watcher

If you are new to bird watching, you may be wondering what you will need.

- Field Journal and Life List —For recording all your observations. It is a good idea to keep it in an plastic bag.

- Field Guide—All the info you need

- Binoculars—Start with an inexpensive set for around twenty dollars and move up when ready.

- Camera—Especially useful when you do not have time or desire to sketch.

- A lightweight backpack or shoulder bag to carry your supplies.

- You might want to have an assortment of sketching or colored pencils.

- Bird feed can be very useful.

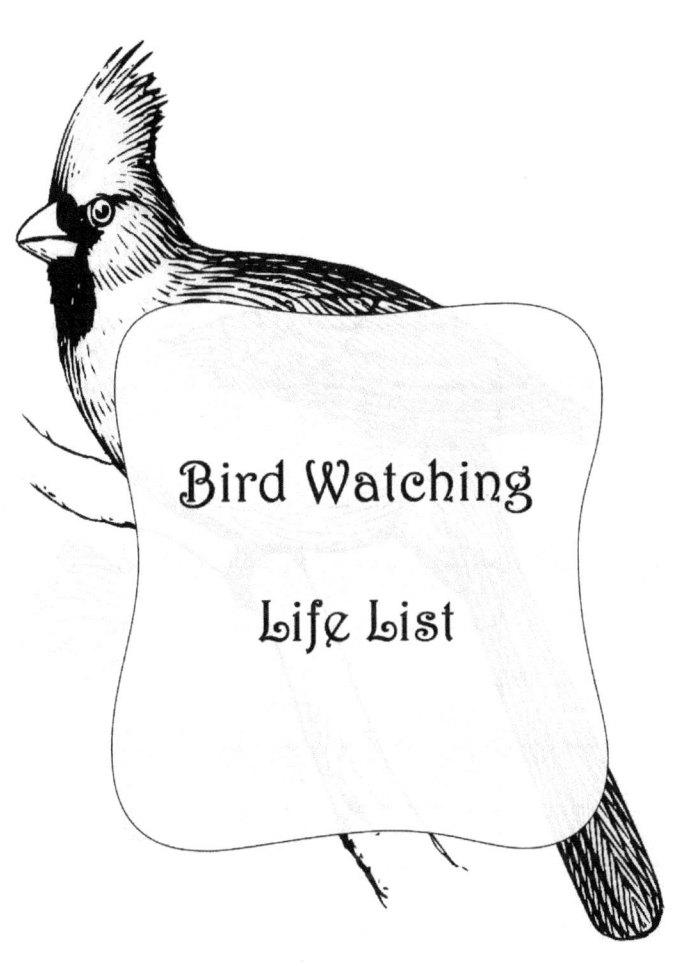

Bird Watching

Life List

Life Sightings

Date	Location	Common Name	Scientific Name	Male Female

Life Sightings

Weather	Notes: Habits, How many, Behavior, etc.

Life Sightings

Date	Location	Common Name	Scientific Name	Male Female

Life Sightings

Weather	Notes: Habits, How many, Behavior, etc.

Life Sightings

Date	Location	Common Name	Scientific Name	Male Female

Life Sightings

Weather	Notes: Habits, How many, Behavior, etc.

Life Sightings

Date	Location	Common Name	Scientific Name	Male Female

Life Sightings

Weather	Notes: Habits, How many, Behavior, etc.

Life Sightings

Date	Location	Common Name	Scientific Name	Male Female

Life Sightings

Weather	Notes: Habits, How many, Behavior, etc.

Life Sightings

Date	Location	Common Name	Scientific Name	Male Female

Life Sightings

Weather	Notes: Habits, How many, Behavior, etc.

Life Sightings

Date	Location	Common Name	Scientific Name	Male Female

Life Sightings

Weather	Notes: Habits, How many, Behavior, etc.

Life Sightings

Date	Location	Common Name	Scientific Name	Male Female

Life Sightings

Weather	Notes: Habits, How many, Behavior, etc.

Life Sightings

Date	Location	Common Name	Scientific Name	Male Female

Life Sightings

Weather	Notes: Habits, How many, Behavior, etc.

Life Sightings

Date	Location	Common Name	Scientific Name	Male Female

Life Sightings

Weather	Notes: Habits, How many, Behavior, etc.

Life Sightings

Date	Location	Common Name	Scientific Name	Male Female

Life Sightings

Weather	Notes: Habits, How many, Behavior, etc.

Life Sightings

Date	Location	Common Name	Scientific Name	Male Female

Life Sightings

Weather	Notes: Habits, How many, Behavior, etc.

Life Sightings

Date	Location	Common Name	Scientific Name	Male Female

Life Sightings

Weather	Notes: Habits, How many, Behavior, etc.

Life Sightings

Date	Location	Common Name	Scientific Name	Male Female

Life Sightings

Weather	Notes: Habits, How many, Behavior, etc.

Life Sightings

Date	Location	Common Name	Scientific Name	Male Female

Life Sightings

Weather	Notes: Habits, How many, Behavior, etc.

Life Sightings

Date	Location	Common Name	Scientific Name	Male Female

Life Sightings

Weather	Notes: Habits, How many, Behavior, etc.

Life Sightings

Date	Location	Common Name	Scientific Name	Male Female

Life Sightings

Weather	Notes: Habits, How many, Behavior, etc.

Life Sightings

Date	Location	Common Name	Scientific Name	Male Female

Life Sightings

Weather	Notes: Habits, How many, Behavior, etc.

Life Sightings

Date	Location	Common Name	Scientific Name	Male Female

Life Sightings

Weather	Notes: Habits, How many, Behavior, etc.

Life Sightings

Date	Location	Common Name	Scientific Name	Male Female

Life Sightings

Weather	Notes: Habits, How many, Behavior, etc.

Life Sightings

Date	Location	Common Name	Scientific Name	Male Female

Life Sightings

Weather	Notes: Habits, How many, Behavior, etc.

Life Sightings

Date	Location	Common Name	Scientific Name	Male Female

Life Sightings

Weather	Notes: Habits, How many, Behavior, etc.

Life Sightings

Date	Location	Common Name	Scientific Name	Male Female

Life Sightings

Weather	Notes: Habits, How many, Behavior, etc.

Life Sightings

Date	Location	Common Name	Scientific Name	Male Female

Life Sightings

Weather	Notes: Habits, How many, Behavior, etc.

Life Sightings

Date	Location	Common Name	Scientific Name	Male Female

Life Sightings

Weather	Notes: Habits, How many, Behavior, etc.

Life Sightings

Date	Location	Common Name	Scientific Name	Male Female

Life Sightings

Weather	Notes: Habits, How many, Behavior, etc.

Life Sightings

Date	Location	Common Name	Scientific Name	Male Female

Life Sightings

Weather	Notes: Habits, How many, Behavior, etc.

Life Sightings

Date	Location	Common Name	Scientific Name	Male Female

Life Sightings

Weather	Notes: Habits, How many, Behavior, etc.

Life Sightings

Date	Location	Common Name	Scientific Name	Male Female

Life Sightings

Weather	Notes: Habits, How many, Behavior, etc.

Life Sightings

Date	Location	Common Name	Scientific Name	Male Female

Life Sightings

Weather	Notes: Habits, How many, Behavior, etc.

Life Sightings

Date	Location	Common Name	Scientific Name	Male Female

Life Sightings

Weather	Notes: Habits, How many, Behavior, etc.

Life Sightings

Date	Location	Common Name	Scientific Name	Male Female

Life Sightings

Weather	Notes: Habits, How many, Behavior, etc.

Life Sightings

Date	Location	Common Name	Scientific Name	Male Female

Life Sightings

Weather	Notes: Habits, How many, Behavior, etc.

Life Sightings

Date	Location	Common Name	Scientific Name	Male Female

Life Sightings

Weather	Notes: Habits, How many, Behavior, etc.

Bird Watching

Yard List

My Yard Sightings

Date	Location	Common Name	Scientific Name	Male Female

My Yard Sightings

Weather	Notes: Habits, How many, Behavior, etc.

My Yard Sightings

Date	Location	Common Name	Scientific Name	Male Female

My Yard Sightings

Weather	Notes: Habits, How many, Behavior, etc.

My Yard Sightings

Date	Location	Common Name	Scientific Name	Male Female

My Yard Sightings

Weather	Notes: Habits, How many, Behavior, etc.

My Yard Sightings

Date	Location	Common Name	Scientific Name	Male Female

My Yard Sightings

Weather	Notes: Habits, How many, Behavior, etc.

My Yard Sightings

Date	Location	Common Name	Scientific Name	Male Female

My Yard Sightings

Weather	Notes: Habits, How many, Behavior, etc.

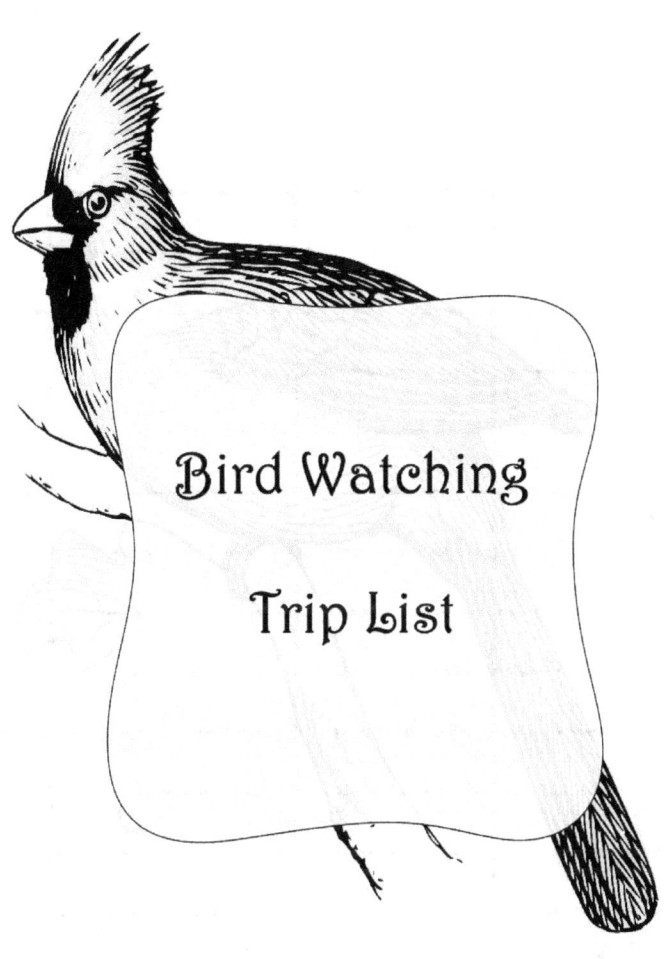

Bird Watching

Trip List

Trip Sightings

Date	Location	Common Name	Scientific Name	Male Female

Trip Sightings

Weather	Notes: Habits, How many, Behavior, etc.

Trip Sightings

Date	Location	Common Name	Scientific Name	Male Female

Trip Sightings

Weather	Notes: Habits, How many, Behavior, etc.

Trip Sightings

Date	Location	Common Name	Scientific Name	Male Female

Trip Sightings

Weather	Notes: Habits, How many, Behavior, etc.

Trip Sightings

Date	Location	Common Name	Scientific Name	Male Female

Trip Sightings

Weather	Notes: Habits, How many, Behavior, etc.

Trip Sightings

Date	Location	Common Name	Scientific Name	Male Female

Trip Sightings

Weather	Notes: Habits, How many, Behavior, etc.

Bird Watching

Wish List

Sightings I Wish For

Common Name	Scientific Name	Location	Date Seen

Sightings I Wish For

Common Name	Scientific Name	Location	Date Seen

Sightings I Wish For

Common Name	Scientific Name	Location	Date Seen

Sightings I Wish For

Common Name	Scientific Name	Location	Date Seen

Sightings I Wish For

Common Name	Scientific Name	Location	Date Seen

Sightings I Wish For

Common Name	Scientific Name	Location	Date Seen

Sightings I Wish For

Common Name	Scientific Name	Location	Date Seen

Sightings I Wish For

Common Name	Scientific Name	Location	Date Seen

Sightings I Wish For

Common Name	Scientific Name	Location	Date Seen

Sightings I Wish For

Common Name	Scientific Name	Location	Date Seen

Field Notes

Field Notes

Field Notes

Field Notes

Field Notes

Field Notes

Field Notes

Field Notes

Field Notes

Field Notes

Watch for Other Books in This Series.

Bird Watching: Field Journal
Sea Shell Collecting: Field Journal
Butterfly Observations: Field Journal
Nature Walk: Field Journal

If you like this journal, please be sure to post an evaluation on Amazon and at kimmariejohnson.net.

SOMETHING BEAUTIFUL

Is about to happen. . .

Something Beautiful
by
Kim Marie Johnson

Visit my Blogs
www.kimmariejohnson.net
www.somethingbeautiful.weebly.com
www.mywisteriacottage.weebly.com
www.aggressivelyseekinggod.weebly.com

somethingbeautiful@elberton.net

Kim Marie Johnson is a writer, artist, and designer,. She holds a BFA in Interior Design from UGA and has been designing interiors for more than 25 years. She is also a professional organizer, teacher and speaker. Most important to her is her relationship with God, her three children and five grandchildren who inspire her every second of every day.

www.ingramcontent.com/pod-product-compliance
Lightning Source LLC
Chambersburg PA
CBHW060632290526
45793CB00001B/221